I0109094

THE
TOWN
OF
METHUEN

Massachusetts

In Nineteen Hundred and Three

PICTORIAL
SOUVENIR

An Up-to-Date Booklet, for the Visitor,
the Resident, and for Transmission to
show something of Methuen, one of the
Most Attractive Suburban Towns of the
Old Bay State

SicPress 2013
Methuen, Mass.

The Town of Methuen, Massachusetts In Nineteen Hundred and Three: Pictorial Suouvenir An Up-to-Date Booklet, for the Visitor, the Resident, and for Transmission to show something of Methuen, one of the Most Attractive Suburban Towns of the Old Bay State was originally published in 1903 by the Methuen Transcript, Co., Publishers.

©2013 SicPress.com

14 Pleasant St.

Methuen, Massachusetts.

sales@sicpress.com

METHUEN

The old town of Methuen, one of the richest and most beautiful in all New England, has made remarkable progress as an attractive residential town during recent years. Nature endowed this town generously, and it has been the good fortune of Methuen to possess as citizens certain persons of wealth and large public spirit, who have given without measure toward the creation of those things which today constitute the distinctive features of a beautiful town.

The Early Settlement.

The native inhabitants of the valley of the Merrimack were the Penacook or Pawtucket Indians, of whom the Chief was Passaconnaway, always a friend of the settlers. The greater part of Methuen was at first included in the town of Haverhill. The town was first settled in 1640, by about a dozen colonists from Newbury. Two years later the whole territory was purchased from the Indians, and the original deed is now in the possession of the city of Haverhill. No regular survey was made until 1666. At this time the western boundary extended to a point a mile or two west of Salem village. This boundary remained unchanged until Methuen was set off sixty years afterwards. Between 1666 and 1683 land was set off to different individuals, the lots including land which is now occupied by the east part of Methuen.

SPICKET FALLS

No record can be found showing when or by whom the first settlement was made within the limits of Methuen. It is certain, however, that the east and south parts of the town, near the river, were first occupied, doubtless because they were nearer the towns of Haverhill and Andover. It seems doubtful whether there were many settlers in Methuen until the time it was set off from Haverhill. It is likely that the Indian troubles which extended over many years previous to 1720, seriously checked, if they did not entirely prevent, the settlement on farms.

In 1727,a petition was presented to the town of Haverhill by persons living in what is now Methuen, to be set off as a separate town or parish. This petition Was not granted. A year later the town of Haverhill granted a petition submitted by twenty-seven persons to set off fifty or sixty acres, together with a piece of land lying on a hill commonly known as "Meetinghouse Hill," intimes past.

This did not serve to make the petitioners less a intent on a separation and soon after inhabitants of the western part of Haverhill petitioned the General Court for an act to incorporate them into a town.

THE FIRST TOWN MEETING.

The act passed in December, 1725, and the part to be set off was to be known as the town of Methuen. It was ordered by the court that Stephen Barker, a principal inhabitant of the town of Methuen, be empowered and directed to notify and summons the inhabitants of the said town, duly quali?ed for voters, to assemble sometime in the month of March, next, to choose town officers, according to law, to stand for the year. In

compliance with this order a meeting was appointed for theninth of March, and on this day the first town meeting of Methuen was held. Stephen Barker was moderator and William Whittier was elected town clerk for the ensuing year. The selectmen elected were John Bailey, Ebenezer Barker, Asie Swan, Daniel Bodwell and Thomas Whittier. At this meeting a constable was also elected and minor offices were filled.

GROWTH OF THE TOWN.

After Methuen had been incorporated half a century, the Colonial census showed that the inhabitants numbered 1,326. The old tax book of that year gives the names of 252 poll tax payers. Year by year the town has grown, not alone in population, but also in other respects. It now has a population of about 8,000 people, and over 2,100 poll tax payers.

GOOD ROADS.

Methuen has many miles of excellent macadamifzed streets which are acknowledged to be superior to those of any town or city in this section of New England. In addition to the practical bene?ts derived by the towns people from these good roads, there is a special attraction in them for the riding public of this town, and the neighboring city and towns. In the summer season the

ALONG THE SPICKET

streets are beautifully shaded by handsome trees, which add much to the attractiveness of the town. A great deal has been done in Methuen for the protection and development of tree beauty. One citizen alone has furnished several thousand trees to the public free of cost, and he has had thousands more planted about his numerous properties.

WATER SUPPLY.

Methuen has gained a high reputation for its fine system of water works. The plant is a substantial one and the bene?ts received are greatly appreciated by the townspeople. There has never been any sickness in a first-class fire department which has the proper appliances to work with. It has an up-to-date hose wagon, swing harnesses attached, drawn by a handsome pair of horses, an up-to-date hook and ladder truck also drawn by two horses, and a first-class steamer held in reserve. There is an extensive fire alarm system, with a large number of call boxes. A central fire station, fully up-to-date in all its appointments, furnishes an excellent home for the fire department.

THE NEVINS MEMORIAL.

The Nevins Memorial library and hall, with its beautiful surroundings, attracts the eye from a distance as being a magnificent structure. Before entering the building one is charmed by the beautifully laid out grounds, on which, in the rear of the building, is a beautiful monument erected to the memory of Mr. and Mrs. David Nevins. Upon entering the library one finds a never ending supply of standard literature. The towns-people have the free use of the volumes contained therein, and in addition to this a handsome reading room, provided with all of the high grade papers and magazines, is kept open for all who choose to use it. The library and reading room are, without exception, the finest in any town or city in this vicinity. The hall which is used for select entertainments only is not surpassed in beauty anywhere in New England. It has a seating capacity of over five hundred.

CHURCHES.

The largest church in this town is the Congregagational. This is a handsome edifice, as also is Phillips Chapel, which adjoins it. Both are surrounded by handsome grounds. In the church is a handsome memorial window set in the rear of a beautiful apse. The window has no superior in the country. The subject is the "Resurrection." There are five life size figures in the window—Christ and four angels. The whole picture, composed of about ten thousand pieces of glass, is rich with splendor of colors. It is the master-piece of Mr. John LaFarge of New York, and the cost of the entire memorial was about $60,000, to which was added an exquisite Communion service of silver and gold set with car-

SAND'S BRIDGE

buncles. The window and the apse were erected in memory of Col. Henry C. Nevins, by his Widow.

Through the generosity of Mr. Charles H. Tenney, the Universalist church was recently remodelled. It is now known as the Gleason Memorial Universalist Church. The interior is especially handsome.

One of the prettiest and most unique church buildings to be found anywhere, is that of the Second Primitive Methodist Church, which was constructed for this society two years ago by Mr. E. F. Searles. The work was all done in the most thorough manner.

In addition to these churches there are also the Baptist, Methodist and St. Thomas.

PUBLIC SCHOOLS.

Methuen is well supplied with public schools and they are in charge of an able superintendent and school committee. A very efficient corps of teachers is employed in the schools, and as a result good work is accomplished, and the children of Methuen receive all the bene?ts that can possibly be derived from public school education. Methuen has been very liberal in building modern school housels." The high school is soon to have a new home in the handsome building erected by Mr. E. F. Searles. An illustration appears in this book.

CLUB HOUSE.

The Methuen Club has an exceptionally fine home. This building, which was once a hotel, was a few years ago entirely remodelled, at great expense, by the gentleman referred to in the preceding paragraph, and the club members now derive special enjoyment from these attractive quarters.

THE WASHINGTON MONUMENT.

This diginified and impressive monumental work the crowning achievement of the veteran American sculptor, Thomas Ball, was made in Florence on a commission given by Edward F. Searles, and occupied the sculptor's time for several years. It is of Washington who is represented as a standing ?gure some fifteen feet in height, on a shaft of white Carrara marble rising from a base of the same material. On each of the four corners of the monument is a figure typifying respectively "Oppression," "Revolution," "Victory" and "Peace." These with the Washington are all of bronze, and are most effective. In niches are portrait busts of the revolutionary generals, Lincoln, Knox, Greene and LaFayette, all capital likenesses. The monument stands in Washington Park.

THE SOLDIERS' MONUMENT.

This monument stands at the junction of Pleasant and Charles streets, and is a model of taste in every respect. The material in its construction is principally Hallowell granite. On the east side is , inscribed, "To the Soldiers and Sailors who fought in defense of the Union," and on the opposite side, " Presented by C. H. Tenney, 1888." Midway between the base and the top on the north and south sides, are two lions, cut in granite, one, on the north, in an attitude of repose, and the other appearing as if in anger; under the latter is cut 1861, while beneath the first 1865 is placed. This feature is very appropriate as illustrating the feeling at those times. At the top is a sphere of polished Quincy granite, surmounted by a large bronze eagle with wings outstretched. The height from base to summit is 32 feet 4 inches.

On a triangular plot just to the east of the Soldiers' Monument is the D. A. . Boulder, erected June 17, 1903, to the memory of the Revolutionary Soldiers of Methuen.

Handsome Estates.

There are in Methuen three large and handsome estates. "Pine Lodge" is the oldest estate, dating back nearly one hundred years. It is the residence of Mr. E. F. Searles, one of the town's most public-spirited citizens. This estate is particularly notable for its massive stone walls and grand towers. "Grey Court" is the beautiful estate of Mr. Charles H. Tenney. The handsome stone house crowns the summit of one of the highest hills in the town. Leading to the mansion from the public thoroughfare is a driveway shaded with handsome trees and beautified by shrubs of various descriptions. The grounds' and avenues surrounding this beautiful residence are grand. Mr. Tenney has contributed generously toward the beautifying of the town.

The Nevins Estate has long been a point of interest to the townspeople and visitors. The spacious lawns, handsome trees and shrubs, all kept with the utmost care, are greatly admired. The Nevins family have ever had the welfare of Methuen at heart. It was from this town that David Nevins started out to seek his fortune, and how well he succeeded is known to all. To his sons, David and Henry C. (both now deceased), Methuen today owes a large share of its attractiveness.

An Ideal Residential Town.

Methuen certainly possesses exceptional attractions as a place for residence. The many distinctive features which contribute to make it so desirable from an artistic point of view have already been mentioned. Also the good churches, schools, fire protection, macadam roads and pure water. There are also best modern facilities for traveling by trolley and steam roads, free mail delivery, and easy access to Boston.

On the following pages are shown many of the handsome residences in town. These are simply specimens: there are many more, and the number is increasing rapidly. There are a number of fine modern houses offered for rent, conspicuous among them being those on Central street owned by Mr. E. A. Archibald, and illustrated in these pages. Few towns can present stronger claims upon any person looking for an ideal place of residence.

JUNCTION OF HAMPSHIRE STREET AND BROADWAY

THE NEVINS MEMORIAL LIBRARY

The New Educational Building

14

Washington Monument

15

SOLDIERS MONUMENT

16

Boulder Erected to Memory of Revolutionary Soldiers, by Samuel Adams Chapter, D.A.R.

Congregational Church and Phillips Chapel

BAPTIST CHURCH

METHODIST CHURCH

SECOND PRIMITIVE METHODIST CHURCH

INTERIOR GLEASON MEMORIAL UNIVERALIST CHURCH

21

SPICKET RIVER, BROADWAY AT ORGAN FACTORY

ST. MONICA'S CHURCH

Stone Staircase Between Park and Charles Streets

23

Residence of Mrs. David Nevins

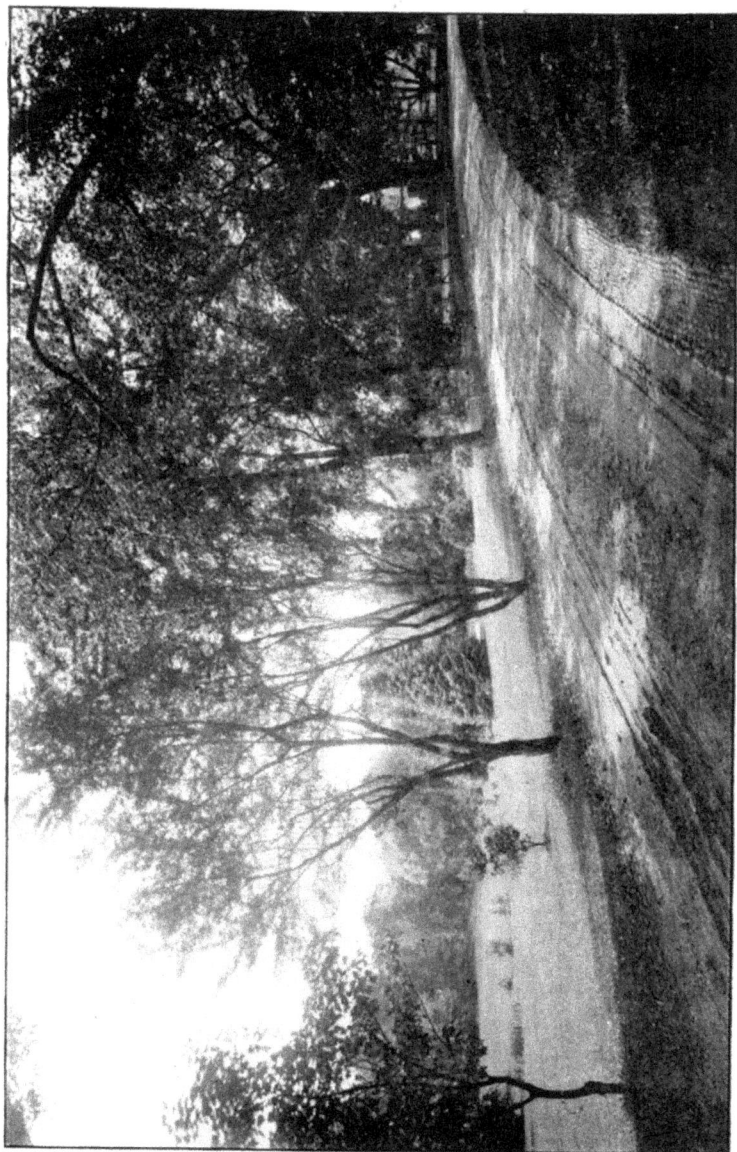

Nevins Estate, from Hampshire Street

Bay Lodge, Nevins Estate

BAY LODGE, INTERIOR

27

BIRD'S EYE VIEW OF PINE LODGE

28

VIEW OF PINE LODGE FROM BELL TOWER

VIEW AT PINE LODGE

VIEW AT PINE LODGE

VIEW AT PINE LODGE

VIEW AT PINE LODGE

BELL TOWER AT PINE LODGE

The Torches at Pine Lodge

VIEW AT PINE LODGE

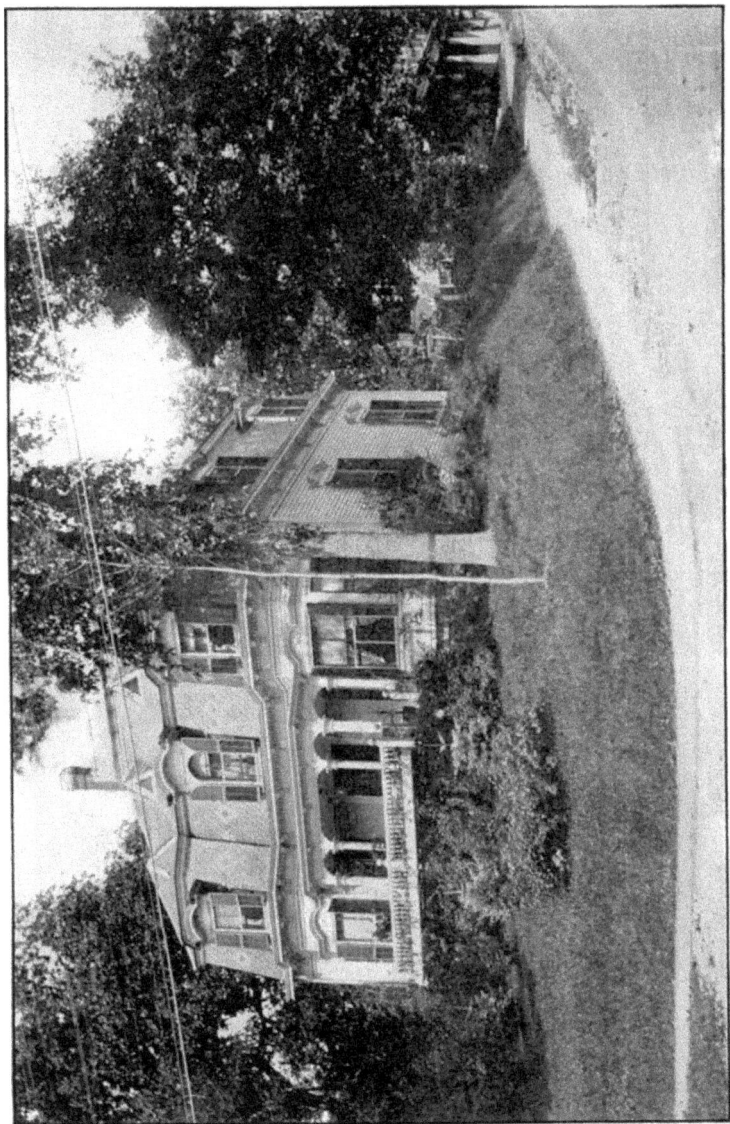

RESIDENCE OF EDWARD A. ARCHIBALD,
SHOWING FORMER HOMER IN THE REAR

Houses No. 13 & 15 Central St.
Owned by Edward A. Archibald

VIEW ON CENTRAL STREET, SHOWING HOUSES OWNED BY EDWARD A. ARCHIBALD

RESIDENCE AND OFFICE OF DR. GEORGE E. WOODBURY

RESIDENCE OF DANIEL W. TENNEY

RESIDENCE OF FRANK REMICK, SUPERINTENDENT KNITTED FABRICS, CO.

RESIDENCE OF GEORGE W. COPP, WATER COMMISSIONER

Residence of Everett H. Archibald, Treasurer and Agent Archibald Wheel Co., Lawrence

GLEASON HOUSE, NOW OCCUPIED BY EDGAR G. HOLT, RESIDENT MANAGER LAWRENCE ICE CO.

RESIDENCE OF GEORGE W. TENNEY

Residence of Charles W. Mann

RESIDENCE OF G. B. EMMONS, PRESIDEN EMMONS LOOM HARNESS CO., LAWRENCE

RESIDENCE OF JOSEPH S. HOWE, TOWN CLERK AND TREASURER

RESIDENCE OF ALFRED SAGAR, SUPERINTENDENT ARLINGTON COTTON MILLS

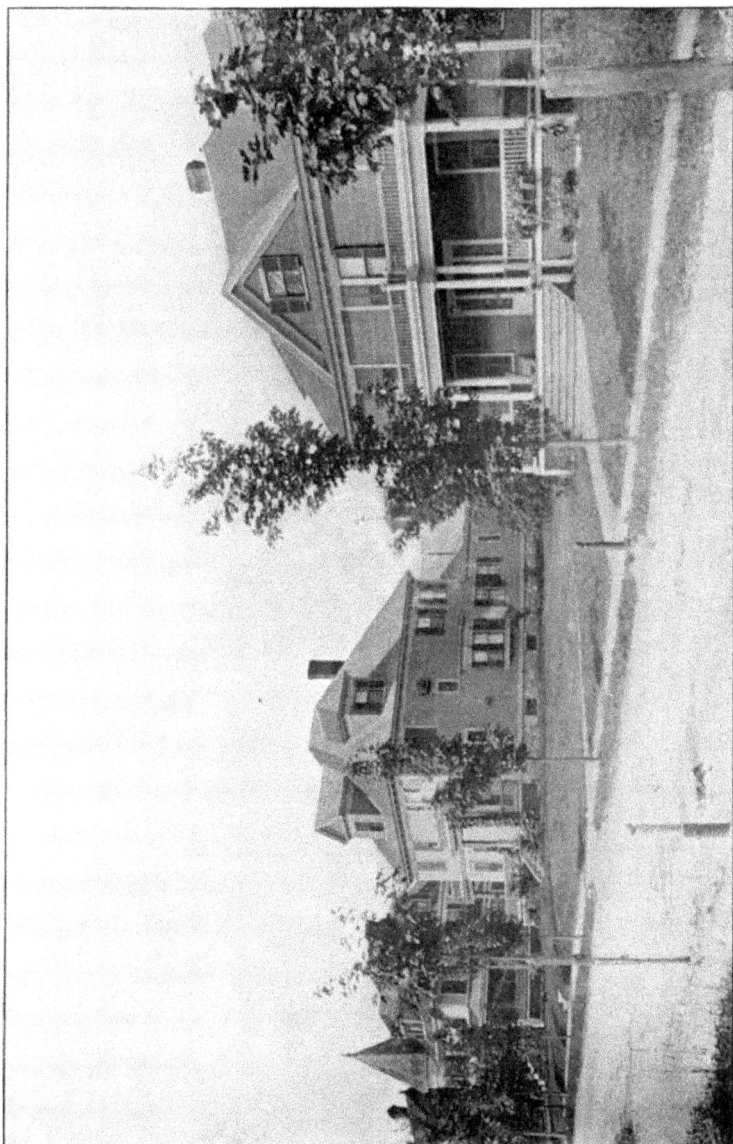

RESIDENCE OF H. E. MOORE, A. E. WHITE, SUPT. OF SCHOOLS AND PETER CARROW

Driveway Leading to "Grey Court"

VIEW OF "GREY COURT"

View at "Grey Court"

VIEW AT "GREY COURT"

View at "Grey Court"

Residence and Office of Dr. James R. Berwick

Residence of W. H. H. Dodge

View on Grounds of W. H.H. Dodge

Residence of William D. Hartshorne, Agent Arlington Mills, Lawrence and Methuen

RESIDENCE OF JACOB EMERSON, CASHIER NATIONAL BANK OF METHUEN

RESIDENCE OF JOHN A. PERKINS, CASHIER MERCHANTS NATIONAL BANK, LAWRENCE

Residence of Urias Hardy, Overseer at Arlington Mills

RESIDENCE OF L.C.MOORE, TREASURER L.C. MOORE COMPANY, LAWRENCE

RESIDENCE OF DR. J.G. MCALLISTER

RESIDENCE OF CHARLES M. BARNARD, EDITOR "METHUEN TRANSCRIPT"

RESIDENCE OF JOSEPH C. BROWN, OF BROWN & WHITTIER, LAWRENCE

RESIDENCE OF HON. JOHN BREEN

RESIDENCE OF ALFRED NEWSHOLME, WATER COMMISSIONER

Residence of James F. Craven

*Tenement Houses on Oakland Avenue,
Owned by Jonathan Craven*

The Tavern

73

Waldo House

CENTRAL FIRE STATION

ODD FELLOWS BUILDING

THE TURNPIKE

HOME OF METHUEN CLUB

Methuen Club Reading Room

Home of Merrimack Valley Country Club

CANOBIE LAKE PARK.

CANOBIE LAKE PARK affords a liberal education to the lovers of nature, students of forestry, admirers of landscape gardening, seekers after botanical secrets, and those who look for pleasure and recreation alone.

Canobie Lake Park was evolved from a virgin tract of forest land and meadow and has within its limits a varied collection of trees, shrub and herb, each of which has an interest for some one.

Canobie Lake Park also offers attractions superior to every other summer day resort. It is an ideal spot for picnic and pleasure parties. There is a theatre in which performances are given twice daily by the highest salaried artists on the vaudeville stage. There is also a magnificent dance hall, dining pavilion, ball park, and a mammoth carousal. Boats and canoes may be had at reasonable hire.

Canobie Lake Park can be reached only over the lines of the New Hampshire Traction Co. Fare from Lawrence, 10 cents; from Nashua, 15 cents; from Lowell, 15 cents; from Haverhill, 10 cents.

Do not fail to Visit CANOBIE LAKE PARK.

81

Dining Hall
Canobie Lake
Park

Pavilion
Canobie Lake
Park

82

View at Canobie Lake Park

Theater at Canobie Lake Park

Arlington Mills, Cotton Department

Knitted Fabrics Company's Mill and Dying Plant

Tremont Worsted Company's Mill – Gaunt Brothers, Proprietors

Methuen Company's Mills

METHUEN YARN MILL, J. W. JOWETT PROPRIETOR

METHUEN COMPANY'S MILL

Methuen Plant of Lawrence Ice Company

FREDERICK & BOWER'S DRUG STORE

STORE OF W. K. EPHLIN

STORES OF EDWIN J. CASTLE

...COMPLIMENTS OF...

L. E. Locke...

LAWRENCE, MASS.

...COMPLIMENTS OF...

E. E. Burnham...

LEATHER BELTING and

MILL SUPPLIES

252 LOWELL STREET

LAWRENCE . . . .

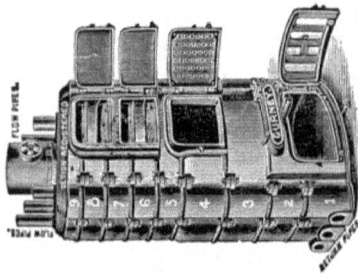

....Are you contemplating making any changes in your

Plumbing or Heating Apparatus,

OR ARE YOU

CONDIDERING BUILDING?

IF SO, ALLOW US TO FURNISH

YOU WITH ESTIMATES

On Plumbing, Steam or Furnace Work and Gas Fixtures

We are agents for Kelsey Hot Air Generators, Gurney, Plummer, and Walker & Pratt Steam Heaters. . . . .

William Forbes & Sons.

450 Essex Street,
Lawrence. . . . .

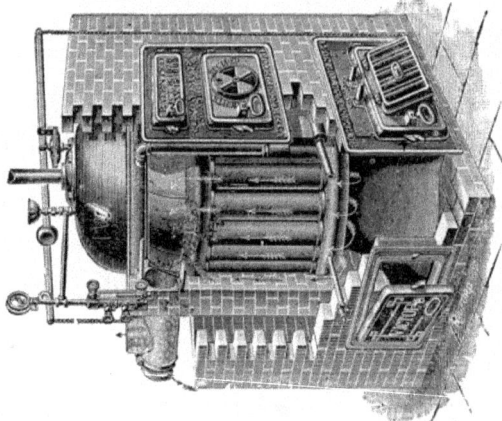

94

THE GAS RANGE will meet every requirement of your kitchen; will make summer cooking bearable, if not actually enjoyable, and will give you more time for rest, for recreation, for calling, or for the enjoyment of your home . . . . . .

CALL and inspect our Ranges. We are pleased to answer questions and may be of some service to you in solving . . . . . . THE FUEL QUESTION

LAWRENCE GAS COMPANY   370 ESSEX ST.

DETROIT JEWEL

95

EVERY FACILITY EXTENDED TO CUSTOMERS
CONSISTENT WITH SOUND BANKING ❧ ❧ ❧

D. W. TENNEY, - - - President
JACOB EMERSON, - - - Cashier
JOHN D. EMERSON, - - - Teller

National Bank
of Methuen ❧

METHUEN
MASSACHUSETTS

Capital, - $100,000
Surplus, - $20,000

Established 1853

Incorporated 1884

BRIGGS & ALLÜN MFG. CO.

...LAWRENCE, MASS.

Fine Interior House Finish
.. and ..
Decorations a Specialty

Kiln Dried Lumber,
Sheathing,
Fence Stock and
Flooring

Stair Builders

Doors, Windows
and Blinds

Gutters and Mouldings

All kinds of House Finish,
Tanks and Vats

Wood Mantels

10 to 20 WINTER STREET
2 MELVIN STREET

Office of the Methuen Transcript Company, Union Publishing Company and Methuen Tage Manufacturing Company

www.ingramcontent.com/pod-product-compliance
Lightning Source LLC
Chambersburg PA
CBHW062011040426
42447CB00010B/2004

* 9 7 8 0 6 1 5 8 1 8 3 8 2 *